Learn to Speak Cantonese 1

A beginner's guide to mastering conversational Cantonese

Jade Jia Ying Wu

Printed in the United States of America
Fifth Printing, 2021
ISBN-13: 978-0-9996946-0-2

To my grandfather,
who taught me how to write
my first Chinese character and
not to forget my roots.
I wish he were here.

Message from the Author

About three years ago, a friend from a business class told me that he was interested in learning Chinese. I told him that I know Chinese and I could teach him. The same day, I went home and created my first website called InspirLang, and began creating podcasts and videos to teach non-native speakers Cantonese, Mandarin, and Taishanese. In the three years since, these published lessons have gained great success, not only through various online media, but also through one-on-one lessons and group sessions in classrooms.

As one of my native languages, Cantonese has always been my favorite. Not only does it influence my daily life and bond me to my family, it is also very interesting in its own form. Cantonese has dominated Chinatown neighborhoods for decades in North America, South America, and Australia. However, one day when I read a *New York Times* article which claimed that Cantonese was dying in Chinatown, I became very upset. I believe that Cantonese deserves its full recognition in both its spoken and written forms as one of the most influential Chinese dialects.

This book is based mainly on my experiences teaching Cantonese and also learning English and other languages. It includes questions that most non-native speakers would ask, as well as cross-cultural questions that most people would raise. I believe that language books can be both fun and educational. When I first started teaching Chinese, I was surprised and disturbed to find that there were very limited resources on the shelf that teach Cantonese to non-native speakers. I hope this book makes learning Cantonese more fun and less intimidating.

You know you are learning one of the most difficult languages in the world, but you also know that the most meaningful things in the world are rarely easy. When you place your first order in Cantonese to a waiter at a restaurant in Chinatown, that is the moment you can celebrate just how much closer you have gotten to someone's heart.

[cin1 lei5 zi1 hang4, ci2 jyu1 zuk1 haa6]
千里之行，始於足下。
A journey of a thousand miles begins with a single step.
– *Lao Tzu*

Good luck and enjoy your journey of learning Cantonese!

Jade Jia Ying Wu
August, 2017

Table of Contents

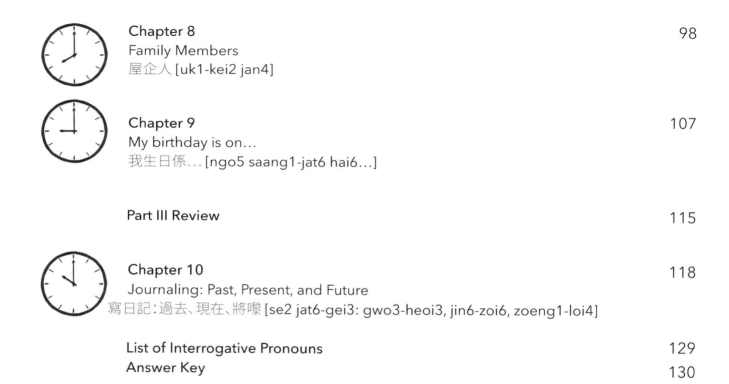

Introduction to Cantonese

Cantonese is the most commonly used dialect in Hong Kong, Macau, Guangdong, and parts of Guangxi, China. It originated in Guangzhou, the southern region of China and northwest of Hong Kong. It has also been dominating Chinatown neighborhoods for decades in North and South America. The history of Cantonese can be traced back to the Qin Dynasty of China (221BC). It is controversial whether Cantonese was once considered the earliest language – "雅言[ngaa5-jin4]" during both Qin and Han Dynasties. There is another reason why Cantonese was considered as the earliest language. The rhyming of poetry from the Tang Dynasty and verse from the Song Dynasty (唐詩宋詞 [tong4-si1 sung3-ci4]) still prevails when read and enunciated in Cantonese.

Although Cantonese shares many characteristics of its grammar and characters with Mandarin Chinese, it has an entirely different Romanization and tonal system than Mandarin. Many characters used in Cantonese are not considered formal written Chinese. Therefore, this book will focus on spoken Cantonese.

Features of This Book

Before you jump ahead and start reading this book, here are a few important features of the book that you should know:

Study Goal

The main goal of this book is to help you to learn how to speak basic Cantonese in the fastest way possible. However, there is a significant difference between spoken Cantonese and written Chinese, so this book does not require the student to learn how to read or write Chinese characters. After learning everything in this book, you should be able to form sentences that are useful in everyday conversation and recognize some of the most commonly used characters.

Audio Track

You can download audio tracks that are supplementary to this book at *www.inspirlang.com/resource* at no additional cost. Audio tracks are provided for all chapters of Sample Vocabulary, Sample Sentences, and Sample Conversation with a sign.

Online Flash Cards

You can review and study all of the new vocabulary covered in this book by visiting *www.inspirlang.com/resource*

Vocabulary

In each chapter, there are 3 sections of Sample Vocabulary (A, B and C), all of which are related to the sample topic. Audio tracks are also available online.

Sample Sentences

Similar to Sample Vocabulary, there are 3 sections of Sample Sentences in each chapter, all of which are constructed using Sample Vocabulary. Audio tracks are also available.

Recognizing Chinese Characters

In each chapter, there is a Recognizing Chinese Characters section with 3-5 characters that the reader should learn to recognize because they are related to the chapter topic and are commonly used in Chinese.

Sample Conversation

Sample conversations in each chapter are designed to help the reader to learn how to talk to a Cantonese native speaker spontaneously by using the vocabulary and sentence structure learned in the given chapter. This is the last part of the audio track in each chapter.

Cultural Insight

At the end of each chapter, you will learn some common Cantonese cultural practices such as eating dim sum and Chinese dining etiquette. That's how you know you are not just learning about the language, but also the culture and its people.

Gabriel

Hi, my name is Gabriel, and I am your narrator and Cantonese teacher throughout this book. I live in New York, and I am 24 years old. I have been learning Cantonese from InspirLang. Most importantly, I understand your pain of learning a new language. Trust me, this book will give you a good start with Cantonese and I will show you that Cantonese is not as intimidating as you think it is.

Jenny

This is my girlfriend Jenny, and we have been dating for about 6 months now. She is 22 years old, and we met in an East Asian Studies class in college. Jenny's family is from Hong Kong and she has tried to teach me some Cantonese over time. She loves eating, and as you will see, most of the time her main role in this book is simply eating.

Jenny's Mom

This is Jenny's mom, and this book is focused on the first day I met and spoke Cantonese with her. There may be language barriers and cultural differences, but you know it is worth the effort and challenge because when you truly love someone, you want to get to know the family and the language too.

Crash Course 101 on Cantonese Romanization

Chinese is a tonal language, while English is not. What is the easiest way to understand tones?
Chinese has so many homophones, which means different words that sound alike but have different meanings. Here are two examples of how Chinese sounds can lead to puns:

4 is considered an unlucky number in Chinese
But why? That is because "four 四 [sei3]" is nearly homophonous to the word "death 死 [sei2]". You see that both "four" and "death" have the same spelling of "sei," and the numbers "3" and "2" coming after "sei" indicate the tone of the character. There are 6 tones in Cantonese. From this example, you can see that same spelling with different tones can indicate very different meanings. See the audio section of the Six Tones on the next page and also to hear the difference between each tone.

Good fortune "福 [fuk1]" character hung upside down

This is a common practice of Chinese New Year. But why? It's because "arrival of good fortune 福到 (fuk1-dou3)" sounds exactly the same as "upside down good fortune 福倒 (fuk1-dou3)". From this example you can see, different words can have the same pronunciation, and yet have different meanings.

How can a non-native speaker tell the difference?

I am glad you asked. In 1993, the Linguistic Society of Hong Kong developed an official Cantonese Romanization system called Jyutping to help foreign language speakers to enunciate every Chinese character in Cantonese, once they learn the initials (consonants), finals (vowels), and tones.

Difficult Initials

Jyutping	How it sounds in English
c	ts
j	y
m	mmm
ng	ugh
z	j

What are tones?

Chinese is a tonal language, which means that each character has a fixed pitch pattern. There are 6 tones in Cantonese Jyutping. The digits of 1-6 after the roman letters indicate the fixed tone of that character.

Chinese Character	Pronunciation	Tone	Pronunciation with Tone	English Translation	Pitch
賒		1	se1	to buy or sell on credit	high flat
寫		2	se2	to write	mid rising
瀉		3	se3	diarrhea	mid flat
蛇	se	4	se4	snake	low falling
舍		5	se5	shelter	low rising
射		6	se6	to shoot	low flat

Can't tell the difference from the audio? That is totally fine. This is just for you to be aware that

1. The numbers above represent different tones
2. Different tones indicate different characters
3. Different characters can share the same pronunciation and the same tone (remember the "good fortune" pun we talked about earlier?)

This can be tricky because different characters can have the same pronunciation and tone. How can you know when it means one thing and not the other? Usually you can tell from the context and the combination of characters. For example, the sound "gaa3" can represent many different characters; however, when it's placed before "fe1," it becomes "gaa3-fe1." Then people can tell that it means "coffee."

To make it easier, in this book, multisyllabic words are connected by a dash (-). For example, in "I want coffee (ngo5 jiu3 gaa3-fe1)," gaa3-fe1 is connected by a dash because it is considered one word: coffee.

What if I use the wrong tones?

In most cases, people will still be able to understand you even if you can't say the different tones of each character correctly. However, there are times when combinations of the wrong tones can make up different words. Just remember, the more you listen, the easier it will be to tell the difference between tones; the more you speak, the closer you are to saying it correctly. So don't be afraid to try even though you are not sure if it is the correct tone.

Chapter 1
Hello. I am…
你好。我係…

In this chapter, I am meeting Jenny's mom for the first time in a dim sum restaurant. After reading this chapter, you will be able to greet your friend's parents as well as introduce yourself.

Learn to Speak Cantonese 1

你 [nei5] = you

好 [hou2] = good; well; very

你 [nei5] + 好 [hou2] = hello

As you can see, the way people greet each other in Chinese is similar to saying "you are well" in English.

我 [ngo5] = I; me

係 [hai6] = am, are, is; yes

我 [ngo5] + 係 [hai6] + name = I am...

Remember the numbers after the letter represent the tones!

Now you can introduce yourself to other people in Cantonese!

美國 [mei5-gwok3] = the United States

人 [jan4] = person; people

我 [ngo5] + 係 [hai6] + nationality + 人 [jan4] = I am from…

Vocabulary A 🔊

美國 [mei5-gwok3] = the United States

中國 [zung1-gwok3] = China

加拿大 [gaa1-naa4-daai6] = Canada

國 [gwok3] means "country," and it usually appears at the end of a country name.

Sample Sentences A 🔊

我係美國人。[ngo5 hai6 mei5-gwok3 jan4]
I am American. / I am from the U.S.

我係中國人。[ngo5 hai6 zung1-gwok3 jan4]
I am Chinese. / I am from China.

我係加拿大人。[ngo5 hai6 gaa1-naa4-daai6 jan4]
I am Canadian. / I am from Canada.

Tip: If you need help finding the right words, simply download Pleco Chinese Dictionary on your smartphone and install Cantonese Jyutping as the language and text as a supplement to using this book.

大學 [daai6-hok6] = college; university

讀 [duk6] = to study

工程 [gung1-cing4] = engineering

我 [ngo5] + 大學 [daai6-hok6] + 讀 [duk6] + college major = I study … in college.

Vocabulary B 🔊

工程 [gung1-cing4] = engineering

會計 [wui6-gai3] = accounting

中文 [zung1-man2] = Chinese (language)

Sample Sentences B 🔊

我大學讀工程。[ngo5 daai6-hok6 duk6 gung1-cing4]
I study/studied engineering in college.

我大學讀會計。[ngo5 daai6-hok6 duk6 wui6-gai3]
I study/studied accounting in college.

我大學讀中文。[ngo5 daai6-hok6 duk6 zung1-man2]
I study/studied Chinese in college.

Do you still remember how to say "I am..." in Cantonese? 我係 [ngo5 hai6] = I am...

Vocabulary C 🔊

世伯 [sai3-baak3] = uncle (how you address friend's father)

伯母 [baak3-mou5] = auntie (how you address friend's mother)

工程師 [gung1-cing4-si1] = engineer

會計師 [wui6-gai3-si1] = accountant

學生 [hok6-saang1] = student

Tip: Did you notice the 師 (si1) after the translation engineering 工程 (gung1-cing4) and accounting 會計 (wui6-gai3)? The character 師 (si1) means a master in a certain field and it resembles the "...er", "ist" or "...ant" in English coming after fields of studies such as "teacher," "journalist," and "attendant."

Sample Sentences C 🔊

我係工程師。[ngo5 hai6 gung1-cing4-si1]
I am an engineer.

我係會計師。[ngo5 hai6 wui6-gai3-si1]
I am an accountant.

我係學生。[ngo5 hai6 hok6-saang1]
I am a student.

Recognizing Chinese Characters

1. 我 [ngo5] = I; me

2. 你 [nei5] = you

3. 人 [jan4] = person; people

Tip: Remember, your goal in this book is to get comfortable speaking Cantonese to native speakers. You don't need to worry about writing all the characters yet. Simply learning to recognize these most frequently used characters in each chapter will help you to learn how to write characters in the future.

Sample Conversation 🔊

A: 早晨! [zou2-san4!]

Good morning!

B: 你好，伯母。我係Gabriel。[nei5-hou2, baak3-mou5. ngo5 hai6 Gabriel]

Hi, auntie! I am Gabriel.

A: 你係做咩㗎, Gabriel? [nei5 hai6 zou6 me1 gaa3, Gabriel?]

What do you do? / What is your job, Gabriel?

B: 我係工程師。[ngo5 hai6 gung1-cing4-si1]

I am an engineer.

Cultural Insight | What you should expect:

1. Bring a small gift (such as tea) to the first meeting with your potential Chinese family. It is a simple Chinese way of showing respect.

2. Eating dim sum is often referred as "drink tea 飲茶 (jam2-caa4)" in Cantonese. That is because the custom of eating dim sum comes from a tea house that also serves snacks, which is similar to the coffee shops today. This is how an ancient tea stall looks like. It usually serves buns and tea.

Chapter 1 Exercise

1. What is the literal meaning of "hello 你好 (nei5-hou2)" in Chinese?

_____

2. Translate the following sentences:

我係美國人。[ngo5 hai6 mei5-gwok3 jan4]

_____

你係中國人？[nei5 hai6 zung1-gwok3 jan4?]

_____

我係加拿大人。[ngo5 hai6 gaa1-naa4-daai6 _____]
I am from Canada.

3. Answer the following questions about you.

    A: What do you study?

    B: 我讀會計。[_____ _____ wui6-gai3]
       I study accounting.

    A: What is your occupation?

    B: 我係會計師。[_____ _____ wui6-gai3-si1]
       I am an accountant.

Chapter 2
Excuse me, I would like…
唔該, 我想要…

In Chapter 2, I am ordering different types of food from the dim sum cart for Jenny and Jenny's mom. After reading this chapter, you will be able to order food at a Chinese restaurant and be familiar with some Chinese dining etiquette.

想 [soeng2] = to want to...

要 [jiu3] = to need

想要 [soeng2-jiu3] = would like

我 [ngo5] + 想要 [soeng2-jiu3] + noun = I would like...

Vocabulary A 🔊

蝦餃 [haa1-gaau2] = shrimp dumpling

燒賣 [siu1-maai2] = shiu-mai; steamed dumpling

牛百葉 [ngau4-baak3-jip6] = ginger scallion tripe

蝦腸 [haa1-coeng2] = shrimp rice noodle roll

Sample Sentences A

我想要蝦餃。[ngo5 soeng2-jiu3 haa1-gaau2]
I would like (a serving of) shrimp dumplings.

我想要燒賣。[ngo5 soeng2-jiu3 siu1-maai2]
I would like (a serving of) shiu-mai.

我想要牛百葉。[ngo5 soeng2-jiu3 ngau4-baak3-jip6]
I would like (a serving of) ginger scallion tripes.

Learn to Speak Cantonese 1

我想要蝦腸。[ngo5 soeng2-jiu3 haa1-coeng2]
I would like (a serving of) shrimp rice noodle rolls.

Tip: "我想要… (ngo5 soeng2-jiu3)" is simply a general way of telling the waiter what you would like to order; however, in most dim sum restaurants, you would have to walk to the dim sum cart first in order to get what you want.

唔該 [m4-goi1] = excuse me (for attention); thank you (for service)

唔該, 我想要… [m4-goi1, ngo5 soeng2-jiu3…] = Excuse me, I would like…

Tip: Remember, you can always use 唔該 (m4-goi1) when you want to say "excuse me" to get someone's attention or to thank the other person for the service that he/she has done for you. However, 唔該 (m4-goi1) cannot be used when someone gives you a compliment or a gift. You will learn more about other ways of saying "thank you" in Chapter 6 later.

Vocabulary B 🔊

啲 [di1] = some

茶 [caa4] = tea

水 [seoi2] = water

When you use 啲 [di1], it is indicated that the noun is uncountable or in its plural form, such as "some water" and "some people."

Sample Sentences B 🔊

唔該，我想要啲茶。[m4-goi1, ngo5 soeng2-jiu3 di1 caa4]
Excuse me, I would like some tea.

唔該，我想要啲水。[m4-goi1, ngo5 soeng2-jiu3 di1 seoi2]
Excuse me, I would like some water.

Table Fact 1 – Subject-Verb-Object (S.V.O.) is the most basic word order in Chinese

As you may have noticed, all of the examples that we have encountered so far are simple statements that fall into the subject-verb-object pattern, and they are very similar to English. However, in sentences with interrogative pronouns (what, where, why, when, which, how), the most basic pattern falls into subject-verb-question. You can take a look at the example below.

Vocabulary C 🔊

咩 [me1] = what

Sample Sentences C 🔊

你 [nei5] + 想要 [soeng2-jiu3] + 咩 [me1] ? = What would you like?

As you listen to this book's supplemental audio track, you may notice that the character "you 你 (nei5)" is often pronounced as "lei5." This is because the pronunciation of Cantonese evolved over time and a "lazy sound" has developed. Many native speakers pronounce the initial "n" as "l." In this book, "you 你 (nei5)" is the only character that is written as "nei5" and pronounced as "lei5".

Recognizing Chinese Characters

1. 想 [soeng2] = to want

2. 水 [seoi2] = water

3. 茶 [caa4] = tea

Sample Conversation 🔊

A: 唔該! [m4-goi1]
   Excuse me.

B: 你想要咩? [nei5 soeng2-jiu3 me1?]
What would you like?

A: 我想要啲水。[ngo5 soeng2-jiu3 di1 seoi2]
I would like some water.

B: 好，你等等。[hou2, nei5 dang2-dang2]
Okay, please wait for a second.

A: 唔該。[m4-goi1]
Thank you.

Cultural Insight | What you should expect:

1. Take the initiative and pour tea for everyone in the family.

2. When someone pours you tea, you should gently knock on the table with your index and middle fingers as a way to thank that person. But a "thank you 唔該 (m4-goi1)" is always a plus. This is an aspect of tea etiquette that has started with Emperor Qian Long during Qing Dynasty.

Chapter 2 Exercise

1. What can you say as "thank you" when someone does something for you?

_____

2. What can you say as "excuse me" to get someone's attention?

_____

3. What is missing from this sentence?

[nei5 _____ _____ me1] = What would you like?

4. Translate the following sentences:

[ngo5 soeng2-jiu3 di1 haa1-gaau2]

我想要啲蝦餃。

_____

[nei5 soeng2-jiu3 siu1-maai2?]

你想要燒賣?

_____

5. Fill in the blanks.

A: 你想要咩? [nei5 soeng2 jiu3 _____ ?]
What would you like?

B: 我想要牛百葉。[_____ _____ ngau4-baak3-jip6]
I would like scallion ginger tripe.

Chapter 3
It is delicious. I like it!
好好味。我鍾意！

In Chapter 3, while savoring the delicious dim sum, I am also having a conversation with Jenny's mom about what I usually like to eat. After reading this chapter, you will be able to express what you like to eat and what you don't like to eat. After trying the delicious dim sum, I want to continue the conversation by telling Jenny's mom that I enjoy the food.

Learn to Speak Cantonese 1

好味 [hou2-mei6] = delicious

You may have recognized the first character 好 (hou2) from Chapter 1. If you still remember the literal meaning of "hello 你好 (nei5-hou2)," you probably remember that 好 (hou2) means "good" or "very." In this case, 好味 (hou2-mei6) literally means "good flavor."

好 [hou2] + 好味 [hou2-mei6] = very delicious

food + 好好味 [hou2 hou2-mei6] = ...is very delicious

Vocabulary A 🔊

呢個 [ni1-go3] = this

嗰個 [go2-go3] = that

For the word "this 呢個 (ni1-go3,)" you may have heard some people say "nei1-go3" instead of "ni1-go3." According to the 2016 Jyutping Word List from Linguistic Society of Hong Kong, both pronunciations of "ni1-go3" and "nei1-go3" are acceptable. This book will be using "ni1-go3."

Sample Sentences A 🔊

蝦餃好好味。[haa1-gaau2 hou2 hou2-mei6]
Shrimp dumpling is very delicious.

燒賣好好味。[siu1-maai2 hou2 hou2-mei6]
Shiu-mai is very delicious.

牛百葉好好味。[ngau4-baak3-jip6 hou2 hou2-mei6]
Ginger scallion tripe is very delicious.

蝦腸好好味。[haa1-coeng2 hou2 hou2-mei6]
Shrimp rice noodle roll is very delicious.

呢個好好味。[ni1-go3 hou2 hou2-mei6]
This is very delicious.

嗰個好好味。[go2-go3 hou2 hou2-mei6]
That is very delicious.

Question: Why don't you need "is" when you describe something is delicious?

When you are describing something in Chinese following by an adjective, such as "this is very delicious 呢個好好味 (n1-go3 hou2 hou2-mei6)", you will see that no copula verb "is; am; are 係(hai6)" is used here. Instead, you will use word phrases such as "very", "a little", "quite," or "not" to place before the adjective to express how the extent of the adjective is applied.

鍾意 [zung1-ji3] = to like

食 [sik6] = to eat

我 [ngo5] + 鍾意 [zung1-ji3] + noun = I like...

我 [ngo5] + 鍾意 [zung1-ji3] + 食 [sik6] + food = I like to eat...

我 [ngo5] + 好 [hou2] + 鍾意 [zung1-ji3] + 食 [sik6] + food = I really like to eat...

Vocabulary B 🔊

菜 [coi3] = vegetable; dish

美國菜 [mei5-gwok3 coi3] = American food

中國菜 [zung1-gwok3 coi3] = Chinese food

廣東菜 [gwong2-dung1 coi3] = Cantonese food

點心 [dim2-sam1] = dim sum

Sample Sentences B

我鍾意呢個。[ngo5 zung1-ji3 ni1-go3]
I like this one.

我鍾意食呢個。[ngo5 zung1-ji3 sik6 ni1-go3]
I like to eat this one.

我鍾意食廣東菜。[ngo5 zung1-ji3 sik6 gwong2-dung1 coi3]
I like to eat Cantonese food.

我好鍾意食廣東菜。[ngo5 hou2 zung1-ji3 sik6 gwong2-dung1 coi3]
I really like to eat Cantonese food.

我鍾意你。[ngo5 zung1-ji3 nei5]
I like you.

我好鍾意你。[ngo5 hou2 zung1-ji3 nei5]
I really like you. / I love you.

Cultural Insights

In Chinese culture, people rarely say "I love you" in Chinese between close friends and families. Saying "love you" or "miss you" to friends can be a little awkward. Therefore, you will often hear people say "I really like you 我好鍾意你 (ngo5 hou2 zung1-ji3 nei5)" instead of "I love you 我愛你 (ngo5 oi3 nei5)" in Cantonese.

Vocabulary C 🔊

唔 [m4] = (to) not…

唔 [m4] + 好味 [hou2-mei6] = not delicious

唔 [m4] + 鍾意 [zung1-ji3] + noun/verb = don't like (to)…

我 [ngo5] + 唔 [m4] + 鍾意 [zung1-ji3] + 食 [sik6] + food = I don't like to eat…

Sample Sentences C 🔊

呢個唔好味。[ni1-go3 m4 hou2-mei6]
This is not delicious.

我唔鍾意呢個。[ngo5 m4 zung1-ji3 ni1-go3]
I don't like this one.

我唔鍾意食牛百葉。[ngo5 m4 zung1-ji3 sik6 ngau4-baak3-jip6]
I don't like to eat ginger scallion tripe.

你唔鍾意食廣東菜? [nei5 m4 zung1-ji3 sik6 gwong2-zung1 coi3?]
You don't like to eat Cantonese food?

Recognizing Chinese Characters

1. 菜 [coi3] = vegetable; dish

2. 東 [dung1] = east

3. 廣東 [gwong2-dung1] = Guangdong; the province of Canton

The term 廣東 (gwong2-dung1) is very important because it is the province where the dialect Cantonese 廣東話 (gwong2-dung1-waa2) came from and where it is mainly spoken today other than Hong Kong and Macau. Cantonese is also known as 粵語 (jyut6-jyu5) and 廣州話 (gwong2-zau1-waa2).

Sample Conversation 🔊

A: 你鍾意食咩? [nei5 zung1-ji3 sik6 me1?]
What do you like to eat?

B: 我鍾意食點心。[ngo5 zung1-ji3 sik6 dim2-sam1]
I like to eat dim sum.

A: 你鍾意食廣東菜? [nei5 zung1-ji3 sik6 gwong2-dung1 coi3?]
You like to eat Cantonese food?

B: 係啊, 我好鍾意食廣東菜。[hai6 aa3, ngo5 hou2 zung1-ji3 sik6 gwong2-dung1 coi3]
Yes, I really like to eat Cantonese food.

Cultural Insight | What you should expect:

1. Chinese elders (really) like to feed their guests with lots of food; it's their ways of caring by making sure their guests are well-fed.

2. If you are too full and cannot eat anymore, it is okay to tell your host "我好飽 (ngo5 hou2 baau2) "I am very full" to politely turn down the food.

Chapter 3 Exercise

1. What word do you add before the verb to turn a sentence into a negative statement?

2. Do you need to use "is/are/am 係 (hai6)" before an adjective?

3. What can you say when something is delicious?

4. Translate the following sentences:

   [ngo5 zung1-ji3 sik6 haa1-gaau2]

   [nei5 zung1-ji3 sik6 dim2-sam1?]

   [nei5 m4 zung1-ji3 sik6 mei5-gwok3-coi3?]

5. Fill in the blanks.

   A: 你鍾意咩? [nei5 _____ _____ me1?]

   What do you like?

   你鍾意食咩? [nei5 _____ _____ _____ me1?]

   What do you like to eat?

Learn to Speak Cantonese 1

Part I Review

- To greet another person, you say "你好 (nei5-hou2) hello."
- To tell someone what your name is, you say "我係… (ngo5 hai6…) I am…."
- To tell someone where you are from, you can say "我係…人 (ngo5 hai6…jan4) I am from…."
- To tell someone what you study, you say "我讀…(ngo5 duk6…) I study…."
- To ask for someone's attention, you say "唔該 (m4-goi1) excuse me."
- To thank someone for the service they have done for you, you can also say "唔該 (m4-goi1) thank you."
- To order at a restaurant or cafe, you can say "我想要…(ngo5 soeng2-jiu3…) I would like…."
- To express that the food is very delicious, you can say "好好味 (hou2 hou2-mei6) very delicious."
- To express that you really like something, you can say "我鍾意…(ngo5 zung1-ji3…) I like…."
- To state that you really like to eat something, you can say "我好鍾意食…(ngo5 hou2 zung1-ji3 sik6…) I really like to eat…."
- This = 呢個 (ni1-go3)
- That = 嗰個 (go2-go3)

Sample Paragraph

你好，我叫諾亞。我係美國人。我大學讀中文。我鍾意食意大利菜。

[nei5-hou2, ngo5 giu3 nok6-aa3. Ngo5 hai6 mei5-gwok3 jan4. Ngo5 daai6-hok6 duk6 zung1-man2. Ngo5 zung1-ji3 sik6 ji3-daai6-lei6 coi3]

English Translation:
Hi, my name is Noah. I am from the United States. I study Chinese in college. I like to eat Italian food.

Sample Exercise

Translate the following sentences.

[ngo5 hai6 gwong2-dung1 jan4]

This is very delicious.

[_____ _____]

This is not delicious.

[_____ _____]

Chapter 4
On Sundays I like to…
我禮拜日鍾意…

In Chapter 4, Jenny's mom invites me to her apartment in Chinatown, and I also tell her what I like to do during the weekend. After reading this chapter, you will be able to express your hobbies in Cantonese along with the different days of the week.

禮拜 [lai5-baai3] = week

一 [jat1] = one

禮拜 [lai5-baai3] + 一 [jat1] = Monday

學 [hok6] = learn

廣東話 [gwong2-dung1-waa2] = Cantonese

Subject + Time + Verb phrases

我 [ngo5] + 禮拜一 [lai5-baai3-jat1] + 學廣東話 [hok6 gwong2-dung1-waa2]
I learn Cantonese on Monday.

Vocabulary A 🔊

1. 一 [jat1]
2. 二 [ji6]
3. 三 [saam1]
4. 四 [sei3]
5. 五 [ng5]
6. 六 [luk6]
7. 七 [cat1]
8. 八 [baat3]
9. 九 [gau2]
10. 十 [sap6]

Remember, 4 is considered an unlucky number in Chinese!

2017年 **1**月

SUN 日	MON 一	TUE 二	WED 三	THU 四	FRI 五	SAT 六
1 元旦 New Year	**2** 初五	**3** 初六	**4** 初七	**5** 臘八節	**6** 初九	**7** 初十
8 十一	**9** 十二	**10** 十三	**11** 十四	**12** 十五	**13** 十六	**14** 十七
15 十八	**16** 十九	**17** 二十	**18** 廿一	**19** 廿二	**20** 小年	**21** 廿四
22 廿五	**23** 廿六	**24** 廿七	**25** 廿八	**26** 廿九	**27** 除夕	**28** 春節 Chinese New Year
29 初二	**30** 初三	**31** 初四				

禮拜一 [lai5-baai3-jat1] = Monday

禮拜二 [lai5-baai3-ji6] = Tuesday

禮拜三 [lai5-baai3-saam1] = Wednesday

禮拜四 [lai5-baai3-sei3] = Thursday

禮拜五 [lai5-baai3-ng5] = Friday

禮拜六 [lai5-baai3-luk6] = Saturday

禮拜日 [lai5-baai3-jat6] = Sunday

禮拜尾 [lai5-baai3-mei5] = weekend

Sample Sentences A 🔊

我禮拜二學廣東話。[ngo5 lai5-baai3-ji6 hok6 gwong2-dung1-waa2]
I learn Cantonese on Tuesday.

我禮拜四食美國菜。[ngo5 lai5-baai3-sei3 sik6 mei5-gwok3-coi3]
I have American food on Thursday.

你禮拜六學廣東話？ [nei5 lai5-baai3-luk6 hok6 gwong2-dung1-waa2?]
You learn Cantonese on Saturday?

Do you still remember from Chapter 3 how to tell someone what you like to eat? Don't worry if you can't remember, there are many times that a word doesn't remain in your brain especially when it comes to learning a new language. To refresh your memory, it is "我鍾意 食… (ngo5 zung1-ji3 sik6…)." Now let's incorporate this S.V.O. sentence structure with more activities!

做 [zou6] = to do

你 [nei5] + 鍾意 [zung1-ji3] + 做 [zou6] + 咩 [me1]? = What do you like to do?

Subject + Time (adverb phrase) + Question phrase

你 [nei5] + 禮拜尾 [lai5-baai3-mei5] + 做咩 [zou6 me1]?

What do you do on weekends?

Vocabulary B 🔊

睇 [tai2] + 書 [syu1] = to read (books)

做 [zou6] + 運動 [wan6-dung6] = to (do) exercise

休息 [jau1-sik1] = to rest; to be off from work

Sample Sentences B 🔊

我禮拜尾休息。[ngo5 lai5-baai3-mei5 jau1-sik1]
I am off on weekends.

我禮拜五做運動。[ngo5 lai5-baai3-ng5 zou6 wan6-dung6]
I exercise on Fridays.

我鍾意睇書。[ngo5 zung1-ji3 tai2-syu1]
I like to read.

我禮拜尾鍾意睇書。[ngo5 lai5-baai3-mei5 zung1-ji3 tai2-syu1]
I like to read during weekends.

你禮拜尾鍾意做咩? [nei5 lai5-baai3-mei5 zung1-ji3 zou6 me1?]
What do you like to do on weekends?

點解 [dim2-gaai2] = why

因為 [jan1-wai6] = because

同…傾偈 [tung4…king1-gai2] = to chat with…

同你傾偈 [tung4 nei5 king1-gai2] = to chat with you

Subject + Question phrase + verb phrase

你 [nei5] + 點解 [dim2-gaai2] + 學廣東話 [hok6 gwong2-dung1-waa2] ?

Why do you learn Cantonese?

因為 [jan1-wai6] + 我 [ngo5] + 想 [soeng2] + 同你傾偈 [tung4 nei5 king1-gai2]

Because I want to chat with you.

Do you still remember how to say "this" and "that?"

呢個 [ni1-go3] = *this one*

嗰個 [go2 go3] = *that one*

In Chinese, a classifier, or measure word is needed to quantify or specify the amount of something. That is similar to the "bottle" in the phrase "a bottle of water," the "piece" in "two pieces of paper," and "pound" in "three pounds of beef" in English. There are many classifiers in Chinese, and they are usually classified by a specific category such as shape and functionality. However, the generic classifier that we have been using so far is 個 (go3), which can be used for people and abstract things. Right now, let us first get used to the generic classifier 個 (go3).

Vocabulary C 🔊

上個 [soeng6-go3] = the last one; previous one

下個 [haa6-go3] = the next one

上個禮拜 [soeng6-go3 lai5-baai3] = last week

下個禮拜 [haa6-go3 lai5-baai3] = next week

上個禮拜三 [soeng6-go3 lai5-baai3-saam1] = last Wednesday

呢個禮拜三 [ni1-go3 lai5-baai3-saam1] = this Wednesday

Sample Sentences C 🔊

我上個禮拜三學廣東話。[ngo5 soeng6-go3 lai5-baai3-saam1 hok6 gwong2-dung1-waa2]
I studied Cantonese last Wednesday.

你上個禮拜三學廣東話? [nei5 soeng6-go3 lai5-baai3-saam1 hok6 gwong2-dung1-waa2?]
You studied Cantonese last Wednesday?

Question: Why don't we conjugate the verb "study 學 (hok6)" when we are talking about an event that is happened in the past?

In these two sample sentences, "last Wednesday 上個禮拜三 (soeng6-go3 lai5-baai3-saam1)" already hints that the event was happened in the past. Don't worry about conjugating the verb with different tenses yet (because technically Chinese has no tenses). However, there are participles that you can add to indicate whether the event is happened in the past, present or in the future. You will learn more about it in Chapter 10.

Recognizing Chinese Characters

1. 上 [soeng6] = last/previous; up
2. 下 [haa6] = next; down
3. 個 [go3] is a generic classifier

Did you notice that the character "上 (soeng6)" is pointing upward and "下 (haa6)" is pointing downward? The beauty of written Chinese is that every character represents the universal forms in nature, and in this case, both characters "up 上 (soeng6)" and "down 下 (haa6)" are categorized as self-explanatory characters.

Sample Conversation 🔊

A: Gabriel, 你禮拜尾鍾意做咩? [Gabriel, nei5 lai5-baai3-mei5 zung1-ji3 zou6-me1?]
Gabriel, what do you like to do on weekends?

B: 我平時禮拜尾學廣東話。[ngo5 ping4-si4 lai5-baai3-mei5 hok6 gwong2-dung1-waa2]
I usually learn Cantonese on weekends.

A: 點解你學廣東話? [dim2-gaai2 nei5 hok6 gwong2-dung1-waa2?]
Why do you learn Cantonese?

B: 因為我想同你傾計。[jan1-wai6 ngo5 soeng2 tung4 nei5 king1-gai2]
Because I want to talk to you.

Cultural Insight | What you should expect:

1. When it is your first time visiting a Cantonese family's apartment, always ask if it's needed to take off shoes and switch to a pair of slippers, because it is a Chinese custom to remove shoes at the door. Even if the host says no, you will get bonus points for asking to show politeness.

2. Removing shoes at the door is a Chinese custom because most places in China have squat toilets (households and even public places). Therefore, slippers will help to keep both the place and your feet clean.

This is what a squat
toilet looks like

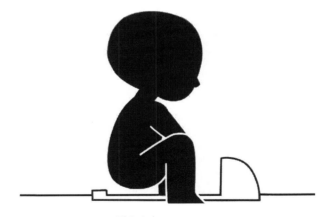

This is how you use
the squat toilet

Chapter 4 Exercise

1. What is the generic classifier that we have been using?

2. How do you say "last Thursday"?

3. How do you say "I studied Cantonese last Thursday"?

4. How do you say "I like to read on Saturdays"?

5. Translate the following sentences.

[ngo5 ni1-go3 lai5-baai3-luk6 zou6 wan6-dung6]
我呢個禮拜六做運動。

[ngo5 ni1-go3 lai5-baai3-luk6 m4 zou6 wan6-dung6]
我呢個禮拜六唔做運動。

6. Can you read the following numbers in Chinese?

[jat1]	[saam1]	[ng5]	[cat1]	[gau2]
一	三	五	七	九
....	....	....	....	....

[ji6]	[sei3]	[luk6]	[baat3]	[sap6]
二	四	四	八	十
....	....	....	....	....

Chapter 5
I work at…
我喺…返工

In Chapter 5, I tell Jenny's mom where I live, where I work, and how I usually get to work. After reading this chapter, you will be able to tell someone a location, a means of transportation, and how to get from one place to another.

返工 [faan1-gung1] = to go to work

搭 [daap3] = to ride; to take (a vehicle)

搭 [daap3] + transportation + 返工 [faan1-gung1] = to take...to go to work

Vocabulary A 🔊

地鐵 [dei6-tit3] = subway

巴士 [baa1-si2] = bus

的士 [dik1-si2] = taxi

行路 [haang4-lou6] = to walk

揸車 [zaa1-ce1] = to drive (a car)

搭車 [daap3-ce1] = to ride a car; to take a bus/subway

Although "搭車 (daap3-ce1)" literally means to ride a car, over time people have started saying "搭車 (daap3-ce1)" while referring to motor vehicles such as buses and subways. When people say "搭車 (daap3-ce1)" instead of "搭巴士 (daap3 baa1-si2)" or "搭地鐵 (daap3 dei6-tit3)," it can be a little hard to know which kind of transportation they are referring to.

Sample Sentences A 🔊

我揸車返工。[ngo5 zaa1-ce1 faan1-gung1]
I drive to work.

我搭地鐵返工。[ngo5 daap3 dei6-tit3 faan1-gung1]
I take a subway to go to work.

我搭D車返工。[ngo5 daap3 D-ce1 faan1-gung1]
I take the D train to go to work.

Do you still remember Cantonese numbers from 1-10?

10 [sap6] + 1 [jat1] = 11 [sap6-jat1]

10 [sap6] + 6 [luk6] = 16 [sap6-luk6]

1. 一 [jat1]   6. 六 [luk6]
2. 二 [ji6]   7. 七 [cat1]
3. 三 [saam1]   8. 八 [baat3]
4. 四 [sei3]   9. 九 [gau2]
5. 五 [ng5]   10. 十 [sap6]

Starting from number 20, you start from the tens digit to the ones digit.

2 [ji6] x 10 [sap6] = 20 [ji6-sap6]

3 [saam1] x 10 [sap6] + 5 [ng5] = 35 [saam1-sap6-ng5]

7 [cat1] x 10 [sap6] + 9 [ngau2] = 79 [cat1-sap6-gau2]

For a complete list of numbers from 0-200, visit www.inspirlang.com/cantonumbers

Vocabulary B 🔊

我哋 [ngo5-dei6] = we; us

你哋 [nei5-dei6] = you (plural)

佢 [keoi5] = he; she; it

佢哋 [keoi5-dei6] = they; them

Sample Sentences B 🔊

我哋搭地鐵返工。[ngo5-dei6 daap3-dei6-tit3 faan1-gung1]
We take the subway to go to work.

佢哋搭M34號巴士返工。[keoi5-dei6 daap3 M saam1-sap6-sei3 hou6 baa1-si2 faan1-gung1]
They take the M34 bus to go to work.

我哋搭M104號巴士返工。[ngo5-dei6 daap3 M jat1-ling4-sei3 hou6 baa1-si2 faan1-gung1]
We take the M104 bus to go to work.

佢哋搭6號車返工。[keoi5-dei6 daap3 luk6 hou6 ce1 faan1-gung1]
They take the No. 6 train/bus to go to work.

In Chinese, adding "號 (hou6)" after a number is equivalent to adding "No." before a number in English. For example, "No. 71" would be expressed as "71號 (hou6)" in Cantonese.

喺 [hai2] is a preposition similar to "at" in English

喺 [hai2] + location + 返工 [faan1-gung1] = to work at…

喺 [hai2] + location + 住 [zyu6] = to live at…

Vocabulary C

紐約 [nau2-joek3] = New York

邊度 [bin1-dou6] = where

大道 [daai6-dou6] = avenue

街 [gaai1] = street

唐人街 [tong4-jan4-gaai1] = Chinatown

Sample Sentences C

我喺34街返工。[ngo5 hai2 saam1-sap6-sei3 gaai1 faan1-gung1]
I work on 34th Street.

我喺5大道返工。[ngo5 hai2 ng5 daai6-dou6 faan1-gung1]
I work on 5th Avenue.

我喺92街住。[ngo5 hai2 gau2-sap6-ji6 gaai1 zyu6]
I live on 92nd Street.

Unlike English where you have to use an ordinal number before street and avenue such as "fifth avenue" and "fourteenth street," in Cantonese, you can simply say "5大道 (ng5 daai-dou6)" and "14 街 (sap6-sei3 gaai1)," which is literally "five avenue" and "fourteen street."

Recognizing Chinese Characters

1. 一 [jat1] = one

2. 二 [ji6] = two

3. 三 [saam1] = three

4. 街 [gaai1] = street

Sample Conversation 🔊

A: Gabriel, 你喺邊度返工? [Gabriel, nei5 hai2 bin1-dou6 faan1-gung1?]
Gabriel, where do you work?

B: 我喺8大道56街返工。[ngo5 hai2 baat3 daai6-dou6 ng5-sap6-luk6 gaai1 faan1-gung1]
I work on 8th avenue and 56th street.

A: 你點樣返工? [nei5 dim2-joeng2 faan1-gung1?]
How do you go to work?

B: 我平時搭地鐵返工。[ngo5 ping4-si4 daap3 dei6-tit3 faan1-gung1]
I usually take the subway to go to work.

你呢, 伯母? 你喺邊度住? [nei5-ne1, baak3-mou5? Nei5 hai2 bin1-dou6 zyu6?]
How about you, auntie? Where do you live?

A: 我喺唐人街住。[ngo5 hai2 tong4-jan4-gaai1 zyu6]
I live in Chinatown.

Cultural Insight | Why is Chinatown called "唐人街 (tong4-jan4 gaai1)?"

Chinatown 唐人街 (tong4-jan4-gaai1), means the street of tong4-jan4, or Chinese people. The reason that overseas Chinese call themselves 唐人 (tong4-jan4) is that the Tang dynasty was one of the most prosperous and successful dynasties throughout Chinese history, from foreign affairs to the governance system inside the country. Therefore, oversea Chinese proudly call themselves 唐人 (tong4-jan4), which literally means "people of Tang".

Chapter 5 Exercise

1. What is the Cantonese preposition that is similar to "at" in English?

_____

2. How would you ask someone where he/she lives?

_____

3. Translate the following sentence:

我搭地鐵返工。[ngo5 daap3 dei6-tit3 faan1-gung1]

_____

我搭7號車返工。[ngo5 daap3 cat1-hou6-ce1 faan1-gung1]

_____

你喺邊度返工? [nei5 hai2 bin1-dou6 faan1-gung1?]

_____

4. Fill in the blanks.

   A: How do you go to work?

   B: 我搭B車返工。[ngo5 daap3 B-ce1 _____]

   I take the B train to go to work.

5. Can you say the following numbers in Cantonese?

   16 _____ (hint: 10+6)

   60 _____ (hint: 6x10)

   67 _____ (hint: 6x10+7)

Chapter 6
How much is…?
…幾錢?

In Chapter 6, I am in a Chinese bakery near Jenny's mom's apartment to order a large iced coffee. After reading this chapter, you will be able to order a beverage at your favorite Chinese bakery and also understand how much the order costs. In chapter 2, we have learned that the simplest way to order is by saying "I would like 我想要 (ngo5 soeng2-jiu3)…." In this chapter, we will further explore how to make an order with more details.

杯 [bui1] = cup; glass (as a container)

一杯 [jat1-bui1] = one cup of...

Remember the generic classifier we have learned from Chapter 4? 個 (go3) is a generic classifier for items.

Vocabulary A

大 [daai6] = big; large

中 [zung1] = medium

细 [sai3] = small

细杯 [sai3-bui1] = small cup of...

咖啡 [gaa3-fe1] = coffee

一杯 [jat1- bui1] + 大杯 [daai6-bui1] + 咖啡 [gaa3-fe1] = a large (cup of) coffee

Let's take a look at a sample menu below.

INSPIRLANG CAFE
飲品 BEVERAGES

Specialty Drinks 特色飲品		M 中	L 大	Hot 熱
Bubble tea	珍珠奶茶 [zan1-zyu1 naai5-caa4]	$3.50	$3.75	$3.50
Thai Iced Tea	泰式奶茶 [taai3-sik1 naai5-caa4]	$3.25	$3.50	$3.25
Coffee	咖啡 [gaa3-fe1]	$3.00	$3.50	$2.00
Hong Kong Milk Tea 港式奶茶	[gong2-sik1 naai5-caa4]	$3.25	$3.50	$3.25
Grass Jelly Milk Tea 仙草凍奶茶	[sin1-cou2 dung3 naai5-caa4]	$3.25	$3.50	-----
Green Tea	綠茶 [luk6-caa4]	$3.00	$3.50	$3.00

Learn to Speak Cantonese 1

Sample Sentences A 🔊

我想要一杯大杯咖啡。[ngo5 soeng2-jiu3 jat1-bui1 daai6-bui1 gaa3-fe1]
I would like a (cup of) large-size coffee.

我想要兩杯中杯咖啡。[ngo5 soeng2-jiu3 loeng5-bui1 zung1-bui1 gaa3-fe1]
I would like two (cups of) medium-size coffee.

我想要三杯细杯咖啡。[ngo5 soeng2-jiu3 saam1-bui1 sai3-bui1 gaa3-fe1]
I would like three (cups of) small-size coffee.

Question: Why do you say "兩杯 (loeng5-bui1)" instead of "二杯 (ji6-bui1)" for "two cups of coffee?"

The number 2 is an exception in Chinese. When you are trying to quantify something with the number 2, you would always use "兩 (loeng5)." For example, when you are trying to say "two cups of coffee," "two people," or even "two o'clock", you would say "兩 (loeng5)." When you are counting "1, 2, 3, 4…," you would use "二 (ji6)."

Do you remember the definition of 要 (jiu3) from Chapter 2?

要 [jiu3] = to need; to want

唔 [m4] = to not

唔 [m4] + 要 [jiu3] = to not want

糖 [tong4] = sugar

唔要 [m4-jiu3] + 糖 [tong4] = to not want sugar

Vocabulary B 🔊

奶
[naai5]
milk

茶
[caa4]
tea

奶茶
[naai5-caa4]
milk tea

珍珠奶茶
[zan1-zyu1 naai5-caa4]
bubble tea

Sample Sentences B 🔊

我想要一杯奶茶, 唔要糖。[ngo5 soeng2-jiu3 jat1-bui1 naai5-caa4, m4 jiu3 tong4]
I would like a (cup of) milk tea, and I don't want sugar.

我想要一杯咖啡, 唔要糖, 要奶。[ngo5 soeng2-jiu3 jat1-bui1 gaa3-fe1, m4 jiu3 tong4, jiu3 naai5]
I would like a (cup of) coffee; I don't want sugar and I want milk.

我想要一杯大杯咖啡, 唔要糖, 要奶。
[ngo5 soeng2-jiu3 jat1-bui1 daai6-bui1 gaa3-fe1, m4 jiu3 tong4, jiu3 naai5]
I would like a large (cup of) coffee; I don't want sugar and I want milk.

As you can see, the conjunction "and" that is used to connect two clauses in English is not so necessary in Chinese. However, when you want to connect two nouns, you will use "同 (tung4)."

同 [tung4] = and

咖啡 [gaa3-fe1] + 同 [tung4] + 奶茶 [naai5-caa4] = coffee and milk tea

幾錢 [gei2-cin2] = how much (does it cost)

number + 蚊 [man1] = …dollar(s)

3 [saam1] + 蚊 [man1] = 3 dollar(s)

Vocabulary C

凍 [dung3] = cold; iced

熱 [jit6] = hot

一杯 [jat1-bui1] + 大杯 [daai6-bui1] + 凍 [dung3] + 咖啡 [gaa3-fe1] = a large iced coffee

Sample Sentences C

我想要一杯大杯凍咖啡。
[ngo5 soeng2-jiu3 jat1-bui1 daai6-bui1 dung3 gaa3-fe1]
I would like a large (cup of) iced coffee.

我想要一杯大杯凍咖啡同一杯大杯凍奶茶。
[ngo5 soeng2-jiu3 jat1-bui1 daai6-bui1 dung3 gaa3-fe1 tung4 jat1-bui1 daai6-bui1 dung3 naai5-caa4]
I would like a large (cup of) iced coffee and a large (cup of) iced milk tea.

我想要一杯細杯凍咖啡, 唔要糖, 要奶。
[ngo5 soeng2-jiu3 jat1-bui1 sai3-bui1 dung3 gaa3-fe1, m4 jiu3 tong4, jiu3 naai5]
I would like a small (cup of) iced coffee; I don't want sugar, and I want milk.

我想要一杯細杯凍咖啡, 唔要糖, 唔要奶。
[ngo5 soeng2-jiu3 jat1-bui1 sai3-bui1 dung3 gaa3-fe1, m4 jiu3 tong4, m4 jiu3 naai5]
I would like a small (cup of) iced coffee; no sugar and no milk.

Recognizing Chinese Characters

1. 大 [daai6] = large; big

2. 中 [zung1] = middle; medium; center

3. 小 [siu2] = small

Note that the character for "small" is "小 (siu2)," which is different than "细 (sai3)" that we have learned before. That is because "细 (sai3)" is acceptable as "small" in spoken Cantonese while "小 (siu2)" is acceptable as written Chinese.

Sample Conversation 🔊

A: [nei5-hou2, ngo5 soeng2-jiu3 jat1-bui1 daai6-bui1 dung3 gaa3-fe1]
你好, 我想要一杯大杯凍咖啡。
Hi, I would like a large (cup of) iced coffee.

B: [jiu3-m4-jiu3 tong4 tung4 naai5?]
要唔要糖同奶?
Do you want milk and sugar?

A: [ngo5 jiu3 naai5, m4 jiu3 tong4]
我要奶，唔要糖。
I want milk, and I don't want sugar.

B: [hou2, m4-goi1 nei5 dang2-dang2]
好，唔該你等等。
Okay, please wait for a second.

A: [gei2-cin2?]
幾錢？
How much is it?

B: [luk6 man1]
6蚊。
6 dollars.

A: [m4-goi1]
唔該。
Thank you.

Cultural Insights | What do you say when you receive a compliment?

Humility is considered as a virtue in many eastern Asian cultures, and therefore it is considered polite to be humble by downplaying yourself when someone gives you a compliment. When someone gives you a compliment, you can simply say "邊度係 (bin1-dou6 hai6)?". Although it literally means "where is it," it implies the speaker's humility by meaning "how am I good enough?"
You may feel a little uneasy when you know you have put a lot of effort to achieve something but have to downplay yourself, but here are two very practical benefits of being humble:

1. To make yourself seem less threatening to others.

2. When you actually make a mistake, no one can blame you because you never claim to be good at it.

Chapter 6 Exercise

1. What is the word that expresses both "excuse me" (for attention) and "thank you" (for service)?

   ....

2. What is the classifier for a drink that means "a cup of...?"

   ....

3. Translate the following sentences:

   [ngo5 soeng2-jiu3 jat1-bui1 zan1-zyu1 naai5-caa4]
   我想要一杯珍珠奶茶。

   [ngo5 soeng2-jiu3 loeng5-bui1 daai6-bui1 zan1-zyu1 naai5-caa4]
   我想要兩杯大杯珍珠奶茶 。

   [zan1-zyu1 naai5-caa4 sei3 man1]
   珍珠奶茶4蚊。

4. Fill in the blanks.

   A: What would you like?

   B: [ngo5 soeng2-jiu3 jat1-bui1 ....]
   我想要一杯凍咖啡。
   I would like an iced coffee.

5. Do you know how to say the following in Cantonese?

$8   _____

$14   _____

$48   _____

Part II Review

- To specify the days of the week, you add "禮拜 (lai5-baai3) week" before the cardinal number, except for Sunday.
- To tell someone what you like to do on the weekends, you can say "我禮拜尾鍾意 (ngo5 lai5-baai3-mei5 zung1-ji3) I like to…during weekends."
- Why = 點解 (dim2-gaai2)
- Because = 因為 (jan1-wai6)
- The last one = 上個 (soeng6-go3)
- The next one = 下個 (haa6-go3)
- To tell someone where you work, you can say "我喺…返工 (ngo5 hai2…faan1-gung1.)"
- To ask someone where he/she works, you can say "你喺邊度返工? (nei5 hai2 bin1-dou6 faan1-gung1?) where do you work?"
- To ask that person how he/she gets to work, you can say "你點樣返工? (nei5 dim2-joeng2 faan1-gung1?) how do you go to work?"
- The verb of riding public transportation is "搭 (daap3) to ride."
- To ask how much something is, you can say "幾錢 (gei2-cin2) how much?"
- …dollars = …蚊 (man1)
- To order a beverage, you say "一杯 (jat1-bui1) one cup of…."
- When you don't want something in your food, you can say "唔要…(m4-jiu3…) I don't want…."

- When you want something in your food, you can say "要…(jiu3…) I want…."

Sample Paragraph

我鍾意學廣東話, 我禮拜六學廣東話因為我禮拜日返工。我喺6大道47街返工。我搭7號車返工。

[ngo5 zung1-ji3 hok6 gwong2-dung1-waa2, ngo5 lai5-baai3-luk6 hok6 gwong2-dung1-waa2 jan1-wai6 ngo5 lai5-baai3-jat6 faan1-gung1. ngo5 hai2 luk6 daai6-dou6 sei3-sap6-cat1 gaai1 faan1-gung1. ngo5 daap3 cat1 hou6 ce1 faan1-gung1]

English Translation:
I like learning Cantonese, I learn Cantonese on Saturdays because I work on Sundays. I work on 6th Avenue and 47th Street. I take the No.7 train to go to work.

Sample Exercise

Translate the following sentences.
1. One cup of coffee [___ ___ ___ ___]
2. Two cups of large coffee [___ ___ ___ ___ ___]
3. Three cups of large iced coffee [___ ___ ___ ___ ___ ___]

A Cantonese friend wants to invite you to an event and she wants to know when you are free. How can you tell her your work schedule and provide more details?

Tag us @inspirlang to show us your Cantonese progress.

Chapter 7
Do you know how to cook Chinese food?
你識唔識煮中國菜?

In Chapter 7, I am preparing dinner with Jenny's mom and she will also teach me how to cook Chinese food. After reading this chapter, you will be able to say ordinal numbers in Cantonese and more transition words to apply them to cooking a meal. In chapter 4, we learned about basic numbers, and the good news is that, ordinal numbers in Chinese are much easier than English once you learn the cardinal numbers. Please take a look at the following example on the next page:

Chinese chicken soup

Recipe courtesy of InspirLang Kitchen

INGREDIENTS

- 1 chicken

- 3 handfuls of soybeans

- 1 soup pot of water (about 4 qt)

- 1 tablespoon of salt

- half a ginger - sliced

COOKING TIME low heat for 3 hours

第 [dai6] + 1 [jat1] = first

第 [dai6] + 3 [saam1] = third

煮 [zyu2] = to cook

煮 [zyu2] + food = to cook...

Vocabulary A 🔊

飯 [faan6] = rice; meal

雞肉 [gai1-juk6] = chicken

牛肉 [ngau4-juk6] = beef

豆腐 [dau6-fu6] = tofu

魚 [jyu2] = fish

湯 [tong1] = soup

Cultural Insights: "To eat soup" or "to drink soup?"
That is a very significant culinary difference between the eastern and western food culture. The soup that we usually refer to has a very rich or creamy texture; therefore, in English we say "to eat soup." However, Chinese soup is usually thinner like a broth; therefore, in Chinese you would say "to drink soup 飲湯 (jam2 tong1)."

Chinese clay soup pot

European soup with pasta and
a creamier texture

Do you still remember how to say we/you/they?

我哋 [ngo5-dei6] = we

你哋 [nei5-dei6] = you (plural)

佢哋 [keoi5-dei6] = they

Sample Sentences A 🔊

第一，我哋煮雞肉。[dai6-jat1, ngo5-dei6 zyu2 gai1-juk6]
First, we cook the chicken.

第二，我哋煮飯。[dai6-ji6, ngo5-dei6 zyu2 faan6]
Second, we cook the rice.

第三，我哋煮牛肉。[dai6-saam1, ngo5-dei6 zyu2 ngau4-juk6]
Third, we cook the beef.

Let's take a look at more transition words.

Vocabulary B 🔊

…之前 […zi1-cin4] = before…

…之後 […zi1-hau6] = after…

然後 [jin4-hau6] = then

最後 [zeoi3-hau6] = finally

Sample Sentences B 🔊

煮飯之前, 我哋煮雞肉。[zyu2 faan6 zi1-cin4, ngo5-dei6 zyu2 gai1-juk6]
Before cooking the rice, we will cook the chicken.

煮飯之後, 我哋煮牛肉。[zyu2 faan6 zi1-hau6, ngo5-dei6 zyu2 ngau4-juk6]
After cooking the rice, we will cook the beef.

然後, 我哋煮豆腐。[jin4-hau6, ngo5-dei6 zyu2 dau6-fu6]
Then, we will cook the tofu.

Vocabulary C 🔊

炒 [caau2] = to (stir) fry

炒 [caau2] + 飯 [faan6] = fried rice; to fry rice

炸 [zaa3] = to (deep) fry

炸 [zaa3] + 豆腐 [dau6-fu6] = fried tofu; to fry tofu

蒸 [zing1] = to steam

蒸 [zing1] + 魚 [jyu2] = to steam fish; steamed fish

醃 [jip3] = to marinate

醃 [jip3] + 雞肉 [gai1-juk6] = to marinate chicken

Question: How do you make yes-or-no questions in Cantonese?

It's a little more complicated than it is in English, so let's take a look at the example below:

好 [hou2] = good

唔好 [m4 hou2] = not good

好 [hou2] + 唔好 [m4 hou2] = is it good

As you may have guessed, "好唔好 (hou2-m4-hou2)" literally means "is it good or not good?" Therefore it is translated to "is it good" in English.

識 [sik1] = to know (a skill or a person)

唔識 [m4 sik1] = to not know

識 [sik1] + 唔識 [m4 sik1] = do (you) know

好味 [hou2-mei6] = delicious

唔好味 [m4 hou2-mei6] = not delicious

好 [hou2] + 唔好味 [m4 hou2-mei6] = is (it) delicious

鍾意 [zung1-ji3]　=　to like

唔 鍾意 [m4 zung1-ji3]　=　to not like

鍾 [zung1]　+　唔鍾意 [m4 zung1-ji3]　=　do (you) like

However, there is one exception to this form of yes/no question, which is "do you have 有冇 (jau5-mou5)?" You will learn how to use it in the next chapter.

Sample Sentences C

你鍾唔鍾意炸豆腐? [nei5 zung1-m4-zung1-ji3 zaa3 dau6-fu6?]
Do you like fried tofu?

你鍾唔鍾意食炸豆腐? [nei5 zung1-m4-zung1-ji3 sik6 zaa3 dau6-fu6?]
Do you like to eat fried tofu?

你識唔識煮炸豆腐? [nei5 sik1-m4-sik1 zyu2 zaa3 dau6-fu6?]
Do you know how to cook fried tofu?

我識煮炸豆腐。[ngo5 sik1 zyu2 zaa3 dau6-fu6]
I know how to cook fried tofu.

By the way you may not want to say "I like to eat tofu" in Cantonese because "eating tofu 食豆腐 [sik6 dau6-fu6] is a Chinese slang that means taking advantage of a woman.

Recognizing Chinese Characters

1. 牛 [ngau4] = cow

2. 前 [cin4] = before; front

3. 後 [hau6] = after; behind

Sample Conversation 🔊

A: 你識唔識煮中國菜？[nei5 sik1-m4-sik1 zyu2 zung1-gwok3 coi3]
Do you know how to cook Chinese food?

B: 識少少。[sik1 siu2-siu2]
I know a little bit.

C: 唔緊要。[m4-gan2-jiu3]
That's fine.

[dai6-jat1, ngo5-dei6 zyu2 gai1-juk6]
第一，我哋煮雞肉。
First of all, we will cook the chicken.

[zyu2 gai1-juk6 zi1-cin4, ngo5-dei6 sin1 jip3 hou2 di1 gai1-juk6]

煮雞肉之前，我哋先醃好啲雞肉。

Before cooking the chicken, we have to finish marinating the chicken.

[jin4-hau6, ngo5-dei6 zyu2-faan6 tung4 zing1jyu2]

然後，我哋煮飯同蒸魚。

Then, we will cook the rice and the steamed fish.

[nei5 zung1-m4-zung1-ji3 sik6 jyu2?]

你鍾唔鍾意食魚？

Do you like eating fish?

B: [ngo5 hou2 zung1-ji3 sik6 jyu2]

我好鍾意食魚。

I really like to eat fish.

Cultural Insights | What you should expect

Eating together is extremely important in Chinese families. In most cases where everyone has to work during the day, dinner time is the only quality time when everyone in the family can get together and talk.

In addition to that, Guangdong (the province of Canton) is also well-known for its food culture. In English people greet each other with "How are you doing?" However, in Cantonese usually people say "Have you eaten yet 食咗飯未?(sik6-zo2 faan6 mei6)?" to greet each other. Similar to English, sometimes we don't really wait and pay attention to the other person answering the question of "How are you doing?" This is the same in Cantonese; the person asking the question of "Have you eaten yet 食咗飯未 (sik6-zo2 faan6 mei6)?" may not be very interested in the answer itself, but it is simply a way of greeting each other.

Chapter 7 Exercise

1. What character do you add before a basic number to make it into an ordinal number?

   _____

2. What is the verb "to cook" in Cantonese?

   _____

3. Translate the following sentences:

   [hou2-m4-hou2-mei6?]
   好唔好味?

   _____

   [ngo m4 sik1 zyu2 zung1-gwok3 coi3]
   我唔識煮中國菜。

   _____

4. Fill in the blanks.

   [___ ___ zyu2 me1?]   [___ ___ zyu2 me1?]   [___ ___ zyu2 me1?]
   第一煮咩?   然後煮咩?   最後煮咩?

   What do you cook first?   Then what do you cook?   What do you cook last?

Chapter 8
Family Members
屋企人

In Chapter 8, I am showing a family photo to Jenny's mom and telling her about my family. After reading this chapter, you will be able to refer to different members of your family and also know how to ask and answer questions that relate to your family.

…嘅 [… ge3] = …'s (possessive)

Mary + 嘅 [ge3] = Mary's

我 [ngo5] + 嘅 [ge3] = my

However, when you are talking about your family members or someone who is very close to you, you can omit 嘅 (ge3). Take a look at the example below.

妈妈 [maa4-maa1] = mom

我 [ngo5] + 妈妈 [maa4 maa1] = my mom

Vocabulary A 🔊

Family Members

English	Formal	Informal	Colloquial
mom	[maa4-maa1] 妈妈	[aa3-maa1] 阿妈	---
dad	[baa4-baa1] 爸爸	[aa3-baa4] 阿爸	[lou5-dau6] 老豆

older sister	[ze4-ze1] 姐姐	[gaa1-ze1] 家姐	---
younger sister	[mui4-mui2] 妹妹	[sai3-mui2] 細妹	---
older brother	[go4-go1] 哥哥	[daai6-go1] 大哥	[daai6-lou2] 大佬
younger brother	[dai4-dai2] 弟弟	[sai3-lou2] 細佬	---

Tip: If you are not sure whether to use formal, informal, or colloquial titles for your family members, informal titles would be safe choices.

Sample Sentences A 🔊

佢係我阿媽。[keoi5 hai6 ngo5 aa3-maa1]
She is my mom.

我係佢家姐。[ngo5 hai6 keoi5 gaa1-ze1]
I am his/her older sister.

呢個係我細佬。[ni1-go3 hai6 ngo5 sai3-lou2]
This is my younger brother.

嗰個係我老豆 [go2-go3 hai6 ngo5 lou5-dau6]
That is my dad. (colloquial)

Now we are going to look at that exception of yes/no questions that we learned in the last chapter.

有 [jau5] = to have

冇 [mou5] = to not have

有 [jau5] + 冇 [mou5] + object = do you have…?

Similar to the sentence structure of a yes/no question that we have learned in the previous chapter, to make a yes/no question about "do you have…" or "have you…," you can simply put "有冇 (jau5-mou5)" together, which would literally mean, "have or have not?"

Vocabulary B 🔊

朋友 [pang4-jau5] = friend

男朋友 [naam4-pang4-jau5] = boyfriend

女朋友 [neoi5-pang4-jau5] = girlfriend

好多 [hou2-do1] = many

Sample Sentences B 🔊

你有冇細妹？[nei5 jau5-mou5 sai3-mui2?]
Do you have younger sisters?

我有細妹。[ngo5 jau5 sai3-mui2]
I have (a) younger sister.

我有一個細妹。[ngo5 jau5 jat1-go3 sai3-mui2]
I have one younger sister.

我有一個細妹同一個細佬。[ngo5 jau5 jat1-go3 sai3-mui2 tung4 jat1-go3 sai3-lou2]
I have one younger sister and one younger brother.

你有冇女朋友？[nei5 jau5-mou5 neoi5-pang4-jau5]
Do you have a girlfriend?

我有女朋友。[ngo5 jau5 neoi5-pang4-jau5]
I have (a) girlfriend.

我有一個女朋友。[ngo5 jau5 jat1-go3 neoi5-pang4-jau5]
I have one girlfriend.

我冇好多女朋友。[ngo5 mou5 hou2-do1 neoi5-pang4-jau5]
I don't have many girlfriends.

Vocabulary C 🔊

屋企 [uk1-kei2] = home; house; family

屋企人 [uk1-kei2-jan4] = family member

邊個 [bin1-go3] = who; which one

subject + 係邊個 [hai6 bin1-go3] ? = Who is…?

邊個係 [bin1-go3 hai6] + subject ? = Which one is…?

Sample Sentences C 🔊

佢係邊個? [keoi5 hai6 bin1-go3?]
Who is he/she?

呢個係邊個? [ni1-go3 hai6 bin1-go3?]
Who is this?

邊個係你屋企人? [bin1-go3 hai6 nei5 uk1-kei2-jan4?]
Which one is your family?

邊個係你男朋友？[bin1-go3 hai6 nei5 naam4-pang4-jau5?]
Which one is your boyfriend?

Recognizing Chinese Characters

1. 女 [neoi5] = female; woman

2. 男 [naam4] = male; man

3. 有 [jau5] = to have

Sample Conversation 🔊

A: [Gabriel, nei5 jau5-mou5 hing1-dai6-zi2-mui6?]
Gabriel, 你有冇兄弟姊妹？
Gabriel, do you have any siblings?

B: [ngo5 jau5 jat1-go3 sai3-mui2]
我有一個細妹。
I have a younger sister.

A: [nei5 zung6 jau5 me1 uk1-kei2-jan4?]
你仲有咩屋企人？
What other family members do you have?

B: [ngo5 uk1-kei2 jau5 baa4-baa1 tung4 maa4-maa1]

我屋企有爸爸同媽媽。

I have mom and dad in my family.

A: [nei5 jau5-mou5 soeng2?]

你有冇相?

Do you have a photo (of them)?

B: [ni1-go3 hai6 ngo5 baa4-baa1, ni1-go3 hai6 ngo5 maa4-maa1, ni1-go3 hai6 ngo5 sai3-mui2]

呢個係我爸爸, 呢個係我媽媽, 呢個係我細妹。

This is my dad, this is my mom, and this is my younger sister.

Cultural Insights

Unlike English where you can simply use "brother" and "sister", "aunt" and "uncle," or simply "cousin" to indicate the kinship, the Chinese culture is very particular about the closeness of the kinship. For example, as we have learned, there are specific words that specify an older or younger brother, older or younger sister. There are specific titles for mom's older brother, mom's younger brother, dad's older brother, dad's younger brother, mom's older first cousin who's a female…the list goes on and on, and sometimes even a native Chinese speaker has trouble telling the difference between the titles of relatives. This is just for you to know, and there is no need to worry about knowing each one of them now.

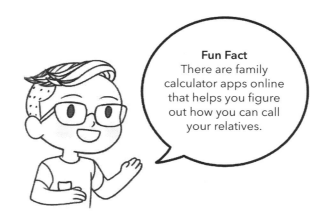

Fun Fact
There are family calculator apps online that helps you figure out how you can call your relatives.

Chapter 8 Exercise

1. What character do you add after a pronoun to make it possessive?

   _____

   Do you need that possessive indicator when you are referring to your family members?

   _____

2. Translate the following sentences:

   Who is this?

   _____

   Do you have a boyfriend?

   _____

   [nei5 neoi5-pang4-jau5 hai6 bin1-go3?]
   你女朋友係邊個?

   _____

3. Fill in the blanks.

   [_____ loeng5-go3 gaa1-ze1]
   我有兩個家姐。
   I have two older sisters.

   [____ ____ sai3-lou2]
   我冇細佬。
   I don't have a younger brother.

Chapter 9
My birthday is on…
我生日係…

In Chapter 9, Jenny's mom tells me when her birthday is and invites me to her birthday dinner later this month. After reading this chapter, you will be able to express dates by using basic numbers that we have learned. You will also know about the culture of Chinese banquets.

2017年 7 月

SUN 日	MON 一	TUE 二	WED 三	THU 四	FRI 五	SAT 六
						1 初八
2 初九	3 初十	4 十一	5 十二	6 十三	7 小暑	8 十五
9 十六	10 十七	11 十八	12 十九	13 二十	14 廿一	15 廿二
16 廿三	17 廿四	18 廿五	19 廿六	20 廿七	21 廿八	22 大暑
23 闰六月	24 初二	25 初三	26 初四	27 初五	28 初六	29 初七
30 初八	31 初九					

歲 [seoi3] = year (of age)

number + 歲 [seoi3] = … years old*

我 [ngo5] + 30 + 歲 [seoi3] = I am 30 years old.

Note that 歲 (seoi3) can only be used for people, animals, or other animated objects such as cartoon characters.

Vocabulary A 🔊

幾歲 [gei2-seoi3] = how many years old

幾時 [gei2-si4] = when

生日 [saang1-jat6] = birthday

Sample Sentences A 🔊

你幾歲? [nei5 gei2-seoi3?]
How old are you?

你細妹幾歲? [nei5 sai3-mui2 gei2-seoi3?]
How old is your younger sister?

我家姐27歲。[ngo5 gaa1-ze1 ji6-sap6-cat1 seoi3]
My older sister is 27 years old.

你幾時生日？[nei5 gei2-si4 saang1-jat6?]
When is your birthday?

你嘅好朋友幾時生日？[nei5-ge3 hou2 pang4-jau5 gei2-si4 saang1-jat6?]
When is your good friend's birthday?

Vocabulary B 🔊

年 [nin4] = year

月 [jyut6] = month

日 / 號 [jat6] / [hou6] = day

2006年 [ji6-ling4-ling4-luk6-nin4] = the year 2006

2017年 [ji6-ling4-jat1-cat1-nin4] = the year 2017

12月 [sap6-ji6-jyut6] = December

23號 [ji6-sap6-saam1 hou6] = 23rd; No. 23

2016年12月23號 [ji6-ling4-jat1-luk6-nin4 sap6-ji6-jyut6 ji6-sap6-saam1hou6]
December 23th, 2016

Question: Why isn't the year placed at the end of the date?
That is due to a cross-cultural difference between Asian countries and western countries. The Chinese culture considers everything in its whole entity, and therefore often emphasizes the big over the small. For example, when Chinese people talk about a date, they go from the year to the month, and then to the day. When they mention an address, they go from the state to the city, and from the street to the house number. As you may have heard, Chinese speakers also say the last name before first name. Just remember bigger units always come before smaller units.

Sample Sentences B 🔊

我嘅生日係12月18號。[ngo5 ge3 saang1-jat6 hai6 sap6-ji6-jyut6 sap6-baat3 hou6]
My birthday is December 18th.

我阿爸嘅生日係5月6號。[ngo5 aa3-baa4 ge3 saang1-jat6 hai6 ng5-jyut6 luk6 hou6]
My dad's birthday is May 6th.

Vocabulary C 🔊

今年 [gam1-nin2] = this year

今個月 [gam1-go3-jyut6] = this month

今日 [gam1-jat6] = today

Sample Sentences C 🔊

我今年46歲。[ngo5 gam1-nin2 sei3-sap6-luk6 seoi3]
I am 46 (years old) this year.

今日係我嘅生日。[gam1-jat6 hai6 ngo5 ge3 saang1-jat6]
Today is my birthday.

我嘅生日係呢個月16號。[ngo5 ge3 saang1-jat6 hai6 ni1-go3-jyut6 sap6-luk6 hou6]
My birthday is the 16th of this month.

今年冇2月29號。[gam1-nin2 mou5 ji6-jyut6 ji6-sap6-gau2 hou6]
There is no February 29th this year.

Actually, there are no verb tenses in Chinese. In the last two examples given, though the translation here is in the present, but it can also indicate the future or the past. Usually it can be understood from context.

Recognizing Chinese Characters

1. 年 [nin4] = year

2. 月 [jyut6] = month

3. 日 [jat6] = day; sun

Sample Conversation 🔊

A: Gabriel, 你今年幾歲? [Gabriel, nei5 gam1-nin2 gei2-seoi3?]
   Gabriel, how old are you this year?

B: 我24歲 [ngo5 ji6-sap6-sei3 seoi3]
   I am 24 years old.

A: 今個月16號係我嘅生日。[gam1-go3-jyut6 sap6 luk6 hou6 hai6 ngo5 ge3 saang1-jat6]
   The 16th this month is my birthday.

   你嚟食飯啦! [nei5 lei4 sik6-faan6 laa1!]
   Come and have dinner!

B: 好呀! [hou2 aa3!]
   That is great!

Cultural Insights | Traditional Chinese Banquets

Traditional large Chinese banquets are generally held for weddings "喜酒 (hei2 zau2)", a child's one-month old celebration "滿月酒 (mun5-jyut6-zau2)" (similar to baby shower but happens after baby's birth), and an elderly person's 60th, 70th or 80th birthday "大壽 (daai6-sau6)." The size of the banquet depends on the budget of the host, and the number of tables can range from as little as one table to hundreds of tables, and one table usually can fit 10 to 12 people. In the U.S., friends and families would usually support the hosts by giving wedding or baby gifts from registries. In a traditional Chinese banquet, it is very common for guests to give cash by putting it into a red envelope and hand it to the host while saying a couple of blessing words in Chinese.

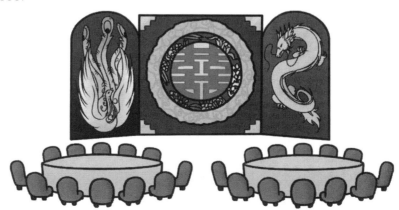

Chapter 9 Exercise

1. What is the order in Chinese to say a date?

   ....

2. Can you use "歲 (seoi3)" to express the age of a building?

   ....

3. Translate the following sentences:

   When is your birthday?

   ....

   My birthday is January 27th.

   ....

   [gam1-jat6 hai6 ji6-ling4-jat1-cat1 nin4 cat1-jyut6 sap6 hou6]
   今日係2017年7月10號。

   ....

4. Fill in the blanks.

   我今年19歲。[ngo5 _____ _____ sap6-gau2-seoi3]
   I am 19 this year.

   今個月係7月。[___ ___ ___ hai6 cat1-jyut7]
   This month is July.

Part III Review

- To turn a simple number into an ordinal number, you add "第 (dai6)" before the number.
- To form a yes/no question, use the "鍾唔鍾意" (zung1-m4-zung1-ji3) structure.
- Do you like = 鍾唔鍾意 (zung1-m4-zung1-ji3)
- Do you have = 有冇 (jau5-mou5)
- Possessive form is: Pronoun + 嘅 (ge3) = …'s
- However, for someone who is very close to you, you can omit "嘅 (ge3)."
- To tell someone your age, you can say "我…歲 (ngo5…seoi3)," adding your age between "ngo5" and "seoi3."
- When = 幾時 (gei2-si4)
- Month of the year = Number + 月 (jyut6)
- Day of the month = Number + 號 (hou6)

Sample Paragraph

I am imagining picking a birthday gift for Jenny's mom.

今日係7月9號, 伯母嘅生日係7月16號。佢鍾意咩呢?佢鍾唔鍾意睇書呢?佢鍾唔鍾意做運動呢?佢鍾唔鍾意飲綠茶呢?佢屋企有冇綠茶呢?我想買綠茶畀佢。

[gam1-jat6 hai6 cat1-jyut6 gau2-hou6, baak3-mou5-ge3 saang1-jat6 hai6 cat1-jyut6 sap6-luk6-hou6. keoi5 zung1-ji3 me1 ne1? keoi5 zung1-m4-zung1-ji3 tai2-syu1 ne1? keoi5 zung1-m4-zung1-ji3 zou6 wan6-dung6 ne1? keoi5 zung1-m4-zung1-ji3 jam2 luk6-caa4 ne1? keoi5 uk1-kei2 jau5-mou5 luk6-caa4 ne1? ngo5 soeng2 maai5 luk6-caa4 bei2 keoi5]

English Translation:
Today is July 9th, and auntie's birthday is on July 16th. What does she like? Does she like reading? Does she like exercising? Does she like green tea? I want to buy green tea for her.

Sample Exercise

Translate the following sentences.

1. Do you like to eat American food?
   [_____]

2. Ngo5 mou5 sai3-mui2.

   _____

3. My birthday is October 14th.
   [_____]

Like Gabriel, you are not a procrastinator and you prepare birthday presents in advance. Write out your thought process as you think about the best present for your Cantonese friend.

Tag us @inspirlang to show us your Cantonese progress.

Learn to Speak Cantonese 1

Chapter 10
Journaling: past, present, and the future
寫日記：过去、现在、将嚟

In Chapter 10, I am writing a journal about the day I met Jenny's mom. I will write about the past, the present, and the future in my journal. After reading this journal, you will be able to use different participles to indicate whether an event happened in the past, present, or future.

Simple Past

verb + 咗 [zo2] = ...ed

嚟 [lei4] = to come

嚟咗 [lei4-zo2] = came

Vocabulary A

Verb	English	Verb with participle	English
[maai5] 買	To buy	[maai5-zo2] 買咗	Bought
[jam2] 飲	To drink	[jam2-zo2] 飲咗	Drank
[m4-gei3-dak1] 唔記得	To forget; to not remember	[m4-gei3-dak1 zo2] 唔記得咗	Forgot
[heoi3] 去	To go	[heoi3-zo2] 去咗	Went

Sample Sentences A 🔊

我今日買咗朱古力。[ngo5 gam1-jat6 maai5-zo2 zyu1-gu1-lik1]
I bought chocolate today.

我今朝飲咗咖啡。[ngo5 gam1-ziu1 jam2-zo2 gaa3-fe1]
I drank coffee this morning.

我唔記得咗。[ngo5 m4 gei3-dak1-zo2]
I forgot.

佢啱啱去咗洗手間。[keoi5 ngaam1-ngaam1 heoi3-zo2 sai2-sau2-gaan1]
He/she just went to the bathroom.

Present Progressive

Verb + 緊 [gan2] = …ing

嚟緊 [lei4-gan2] = coming

Vocabulary B 🔊

Verb	English	Verb with participle	English
[teng1] 聽	To listen	[teng1-gan2] 聽緊	Listening
[zou6] 做	To do	[zou6-gan2] 做緊	Doing
[man6] 問	To ask	[man6-gan2] 問緊	Asking
[hok6] 學	To learn	[hok6-gan2] 學緊	Learning

Sample Sentences B 🔊

我聽緊音樂。[ngo5 teng1-gan2 jam1-ngok6]
I am listening to music.

我細妹做緊功課。[ngo5 sai3-mui2 zou6-gan2 gung1-fo3]
My younger sister is doing homework.

佢問緊老師。[keoi5 man6-gan2 lou5-si1]
He/she is asking the teacher.

Note that 係 (hai6) is not used here before the verb.

Future

會 [wui5] + verb = will…

會嚟 [wui5-lei4] = will come

Vocabulary C 🔊

Verb	English	Verb with participle	English
[tai2] 睇	To look; to watch; to read	[wui5 tai2] 會睇	Will watch
[bong1] 幫	To help	[wui5 bong1] 會幫	Will help
[nam2] 諗	To think	[wui5 nam2] 會諗	Will think
[zing2] 整	To make	[wui5-zing2] 會整	Will make

Sample Sentences C 🔊

我聽日會睇書。[ngo5 ting1-jat6 wui5 tai2-syu1]
I will read books tomorrow.

唔使擔心，我會幫你。[m4-sai2 daam1-sam1, ngo5 wui5 bong1 nei5]
Don't worry, I will help you.

我會諗一諗。[ngo5 wui5 nam2-jat1-nam2]
I will think about it a little bit.

我會整生日蛋糕。[ngo5 wui5 zing2 saang1-jat6 daan6-gou1]
I will make a birthday cake.

Comparisons 🔊

Verb	...ed	...ing	will ...
[zou6] 做	[zou6-zo2] 做咗	[zou6-gan2] 做緊	[wui5 zou6] 會做
[tai2] 睇	[tai2-zo2] 睇咗	[tai2-gan2] 睇緊	[wui5 tai2] 會睇
[hok6] 學	[hok6-zo2] 學咗	[hok6-gan2] 學緊	[wui5 hok6] 會學

Recognizing Chinese Characters

1. 心 [sam1] = heart
2. 會 [wui5] = will
3. 做 [zou6] = to do

Sample Diary 🔊

2017年7月9日 星期日

今日1點，我同Jenny、
Jenny嘅媽媽去听飲茶。

嗰度嘅點心好好味。

我鐘意食蝦餃同燒賣。

然後，我去听伯母屋企。

6點我去听買凍咖啡。

7點我哋煮飯，有炸豆腐
同炒雞肉。

最後，伯母邀請我今個月
16號去食飯。16號係佢嘅
生日。

我覺得我嘅廣東話唔錯。

[gam1-jat6 jat1-dim2, ngo5 tung4 Jenny, Jenny-ge3 maa4-maa1 heoi3-zo2 jam2-caa4]

今日1點，我同Jenny、Jenny嘅媽媽去咗飲茶。

Today, Jenny, Jenny's mom and I went to have dim sum.

[go2-dou6-ge3 dim2-sam1 hou2 hou2-mei6]

嗰度嘅點心好好味。

The dim sum there was very delicious.

[ngo5 zung1-ji3 sik6 haa1-gaau2 tung4 siu1-maai2]

我鍾意食蝦餃同燒賣。

I like to eat shrimp dumplings and shiu-mai.

[jin4-hau6, ngo5-dei6 heoi3-zo2 baak3-mou5 uk1-kei2]

然後，我哋去咗伯母屋企。

Then, we went to auntie's house.

[luk6-dim2 ngo5 heoi3-zo2 maai5 dung3 gaa3-fe1]

6點我去咗買凍咖啡。

I went to buy an iced-coffee at 6 o'clock.

[cat1-dim2 ngo5-dei6 zyu2-faan6, jau5 zaa3 dau6-fu6 tung4 caau2 gai1-juk6]

7點我哋煮飯，有炸豆腐同炒雞肉。

At 7 o'clock we cooked; there was (deep) fried tofu and (stirred) fried chicken.

[zeoi3-hau6, baak3-mou5 jiu1-cing2 ngo5 gam1-go3-jyut6 sap6 luk6-hou6 heoi3 sik6-faan6. Sap6 luk6-hou6 hai6 keoi-ge3 saang1-jat6]

最後，伯母邀請我今個月16號去食飯。16號係佢嘅生日。

Finally, auntie invited me to have dinner with her the 16th of this month. It will be her birthday.

[ngo5 gok3-dak1 ngo5-ge3 gwong2-dung1-waa2 m4-co3]

我覺得我嘅廣東話唔錯。

I think my Cantonese is not bad.

Cultural Insights | Lunar Calendar

Today, most countries in the world used the Gregorian calendar, and that includes the U.S. and China as well. However, China adopted the Gregorian calendar only after Sun Yat-sen founded the Republic of China in 1912. Most Chinese traditional festivals are based on the lunar calendar, because it had a much longer history in China. Well-known Chinese festivals such as Spring Festival (Chinese New Year), Mid-autumn Festival, and Hungry Ghost Festivals are based on the lunar calendar. In addition, the Chinese zodiac signs of 12 animals are also based on the lunar calendar.

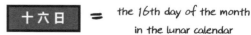 = the 16th day of the month in the lunar calendar

Chapter 10 Exercise

1. Does Chinese have tenses?

   _____

2. Which participle do you add after a verb to indicate an event happened in the past ?

   _____

3. Which participle do you add after a verb to indicate an event is happening now?

   _____

4. Which participle do you add before a verb to indicate an event will happen in the future?

   _____

5. Translate the following sentences:

   I am learning Chinese.

   _____

   I ate chicken today.

   _____

   [ngo5 wui5 bong1 nei5]
   我會幫你。

   _____

List of Interrogative Pronouns

[me1] 咩 = what

[bin1-dou6] 邊度 = where

[dim2-joeng2] 點樣 = how

[gei2-si4] 幾時 = when

[dim2-gaai2] 點解 = why

[bin1-go3] 邊個 = who; which

Learn to Speak Cantonese 1

Answer Key

Chapter 1

1. You are good. / You are well.
2. I am American. / I am from the U.S.
   You are Chinese? / You are from China?
   jan4
3. ngo5 duk6
   ngo5 hai6

Chapter 2

1. m4-goi1 (唔該).
2. m4-goi1 (唔該)
3. soeng2-jiu3
4. I would like some shrimp dumplings.
5. me1
   ngo5 soeng2 jiu3

Chapter 3

1. m4 (唔)
2. no
3. hou2 hou2-mei6 (好好味)
4. I like to eat shrimp dumplings.
   You like to eat dim-sum?
   You don't like to eat American food?
5. zung1-ji3
   zung1-ji3 sik6 (鍾意食)

Part I Review

1. I am from Guangdong.
2. ni1 go3 hou2 hou2 mei6
3. ni1 go3 m4 hou2 mei6

Chapter 4

1. go3 (個)
2. soeng6-go3 lai5-baai3-sei3 (上個禮拜四)
3. ngo5 soeng6-go3 lai5-baai3-sei3 hok6 gwong2-dung1-waa2 (我上個禮拜四學廣東話)
4. ngo5 lai5-baai3-luk6 zung1-ji3 tai2-syu1 (我禮拜六鍾意睇書)
5. I exercise this Saturday.
   I don't exercise this Saturday.
6. 1 3 5 7 9
   2 4 6 8 10

Chapter 5

1. hai2 (喺)
2. nei5 hai2 bin1-dou6 zyu6? (你喺邊度住?)
3. I take the subway to go to work.
   I take the No. 7 train to go to work.
   Where do you work?
4. faan1-gung1

5. sap6-luk6

   luk6-sap6

   luk6-sap6-cat1

Chapter 6

1. m4-goi1 (唔該)
2. bui1 (杯)
3. I would like a (cup of) bubble tea.

   I would like two (cups of) large bubble tea.

   Bubble tea is $4.
4. dung3 gaa3-fe1
5. baat3 man1

   sap6-sei3 man1

   sei3-sap6-baat3 man1

Part II Review

1. jat1 bui1 gaa3 fe1
2. loeng5 bui2 daai6 bui1 gaa3 fe1
3. saam1 bui1 daai6 bui1 dung3 gaa3 fe1

Chapter 7

1. dai6 (第)
2. zyu2 (煮)
3. Is it delicious?

   I don't know how to cook Chinese food.

4. dai6-jat1

   jin4-hau6

   zeoi3-hau6

Chapter 8

1. ge3 (嘅)

   no
2. ni1-go3 hai6 bin1-go3?

   (呢個係邊個?)

   nei5 jau5-mou5 naam4-pang4-jau5?

   (你有冇男朋友?)

   Who is your girlfriend?
3. ngo5 jau5

   ngo5 mou5

Chapter 9

1. year-month-day
2. no
3. nei5 gei2-si4 saang1-jat6?

   (你幾時生日?)

   ngo5 saang1-jat6 hai6 jat1-jyut6 ji6-sap6-cat1-hou6

   (我生日係1月27號)

   Today is July 10th, 2017.
4. gam1-nin2

   gam1-go3-jyut6

Part III Review

1. nei5 zung1 m4 zung1 ji3 sik6 mei5 gwok3 coi3
2. I don't have a sister.
3. ngo5 saang1 jat6 hai6 sap6 jyut6 sap6 sei3 hou6

Chapter 10

1. no
2. zo2 (咗)
3. gan2 (緊)
4. wui5 (會)
5. ngo5 hok6-gan2 zung1-man2 (我學緊中文)
    ngo5 gam1-jat6 sik6-zo2 gai1-juk6 (我今日食咗雞肉)
    I will help you.

References

Cheung, Samuel Hung Nin 張洪年. A Grammar of Cantonese as Spoken in Hong Kong (revised ed.). Hong Kong: The Chinese University Press, 2007. Print.

Li, Emil 李嘉亮. 粵讀粵有趣. Hong Kong: New Talent Press, July 2015. Print.

Linguistic Society of Hong Kong. Jyutping Word List, 2016. Web. 22 Jul. 2017.

Liu, Lening 劉樂寧. "Chinese syntax and morphology." Teaching Chinese to Students of Other Languages. Beijing Language and Culture University. Jul. 2016. Lecture.

Tang, Sze-Wing 鄧思穎. Lecture on Cantonese Grammar. Hong Kong: The Commercial Press, Jul. 2015. Print.

Acknowledgements

Here are so many people whom I want to thank from my heart because this book would not have become a reality without your love and contribution.

To *Jasmine Xu*, for your beautiful drawings in this book. This book would not be a complete work without your work and spirit.

To the *Writing Center at Baruch College*, for the resources provided to me while editing my early drafts.

To *Ruth Kevess-Cohen*, not only for editing this book, but also for your useful advice in order for me to provide as many resources as I can to the readers.

To *Paul Hiller,* not only for proofreading the final version of this book, but also for supporting and encouraging me throughout the making of this book.

To *Alison Cohen*, my lifelong teacher, friend and inspiration, for your kindness and encouragement and making me believe in myself and follow my heart to write this book.

To *my parents*, who will semantically understand the half of this book that is written in Chinese and be wise enough to guess the other half that is written in English: for your unlimited support and sacrifice in this country, so that I could become a better me.

To *all of my students*, for always reminding me that learning a new language as an adult is not easy, and for always teaching me how to become a better teacher and person.

To *Yobe Qiu and Talent Prep*, for offering your classrooms and endless support to grow my classes and universe of teaching.

To *Daniel Jang*, for inspiring me to write this story of Gabriel, and also serving as my prototype of Gabriel.

About the Author

Jade Jia Ying Wu completed her Teaching Certificate Program in TESOL (Teaching English to Speakers of Other Languages) and TCSOL (Teaching Chinese to Speakers of Other Languages) from Teachers College, Columbia University and Beijing Language and Culture University in 2016. She has taught Chinese in classrooms of various sizes and to students of all ages, in both the U.S. and China.

Jade was born and raised in Guangdong, China, where Cantonese is one of the main dialects. She moved to Swartz Creek, Michigan at the age of 13 and spent most of her young adulthood living in New York City. Experiencing both Chinese and American cultures, she was often confused yet fascinated by the differences between them. In 2014, she created her website InspirLang to teach Cantonese, Mandarin, and Taishanese to non-native speakers, and developed her own Romanized system for Taishanese. She currently hosts three language podcasts: Learn Mandarin Daily, Learn Cantonese Daily, and Learn Taishanese Daily. An instructor at CUNY, she is also the author of *Learn to Speak Mandarin I: A Beginner's Guide to Mastering Conversational Mandarin Chinese.*

In her free time, Jade also enjoys learning other languages such as Spanish, Vietnamese and Korean. She resides in Brooklyn, New York.

Website: www.inspirlang.com
Youtube: www.youtube.com/c/inspirlang
Facebook: www.facebook.com/inspirlang
Twitter: www.twitter.com/inspirlang
RSS Feed: www.inspirlang.com/rssfeed

More from Jade

ISBN 978-0-9996946-2-6

Imagine you have found your dream job at a company that is located in a different country, but you don't speak the language of that country. This is the case for An-An, the narrator of this textbook. An-An is a brave panda from Washington, D.C. who learned Mandarin and traveled across the world to Beijing for his dream job interview. In this Mandarin learning book, you will join An-An for 10 hour (chapters) for his first day in Beijing going to his job interview and learning to speak Chinese in a variety of settings.

Free audio and flashcards downloadable from _www.inspirlang.com/resource_

Learn to Speak Mandarin I is available on Amazon for purchase!

Manufactured by Amazon.ca
Bolton, ON